Mongoose

Other titles in the Nature's Predators series include:

Mongoose

Janet Halfmann

KIDHAVEN PRESS

An imprint of Thomson Gale, a part of The Thomson Corporation

THOMSON

————★————
™

GALE

Detroit • New York • San Francisco • San Diego • New Haven, Conn.
Waterville, Maine • London • Munich

© 2005 Thomson Gale, a part of The Thomson Corporation.

Thomson and Star Logo are trademarks and Gale and KidHaven Press are registered trademarks used herein under license.

For more information, contact
KidHaven Press
27500 Drake Rd.
Farmington Hills, MI 48331-3535
Or you can visit our Internet site at http://www.gale.com

LIBRARY OF CONGRESS CATALOGING-IN-PUBLICATION DATA

Halfmann, Janet.
  Mongoose / by Janet Halfmann.
    p. cm. — (Nature's predators)
  ISBN 0-7377-2622-9 (hardback : alk. paper)

Printed in the United States of America

CONTENTS

CHAPTER ONE

Small, Quick Meat-Eaters

Mongooses belong to the animal order **Carnivora**. This is a large group of meat-eating **mammals**. Members of the group include wolves, lions, and weasels. Mongooses make up the family Herpestidae. They are close relatives of the catlike civets and genets. Mongooses are the oldest carnivores. They have been hunting for 30 million years.

Mongooses live in **habitats** ranging from forests, to grasslands, to dry, sandy plains. The thirty-seven **species** of mongooses live primarily in southern Asia, southwestern Europe, and Africa. In Africa they are the most common carnivores. Mongooses are not native to North and South America. In the late 1800s, however, they were brought to Hawaii and other islands to hunt rats. There they **adapted** to their new homes. The mongoose's ability to live in many different places helps it be a successful **predator**. Mongooses in the wild can live about ten years.

Mongooses are among the smallest carnivores. The dwarf mongoose is the tiniest of the mongoose family. It is about the size of a red squirrel and weighs eleven ounces. One of the largest is the white-tailed mongoose. It measures forty inches from head to tail and weighs eleven pounds.

The Mongoose's Body

Most mongooses are long and slender with extremely agile bodies. Their flexible bodies allow them to dodge and pounce with lightning speed when hunting **prey**. Mongooses have extremely fast reflexes—quicker than a snake or a rat. Many kinds of mongooses can change direction in full flight. The slender mongoose (which is a type of mongoose) often does this by leaping at and bouncing off trees. The small dwarf mongooses are narrow and flexible enough to pursue mice and other prey right into their **burrows**.

The legs of most mongooses are short, to help them hunt along the ground. Despite having short legs most mongooses can run fast over short distances. Some can even run backward surprisingly fast. Mongoose legs are also strong and flexible for making quick movements when hunting prey or fleeing predators. Some mongooses, such as the slender mongoose and dwarf mongoose, can leap three feet into the air to grab a flying insect.

Mongooses have small and agile bodies and they have incredibly fast reflexes.

Mongoose feet are narrow with long, strong claws on the toes. The front claws are especially long. Toes and claws are adapted for digging prey from the ground and for digging burrows. Mongooses also use the front paws for picking up food such as eggs. Sometimes, they hold onto prey with their paws while eating.

The tails of most mongooses are long and bushy. They use their muscular tails to balance themselves when they rear up on their hind legs. Mongooses often stand upright to search for prey or enemies.

Keen Senses

Mongooses have keen senses that make them extremely alert to prey and predators. Above all, mongooses rely on their noses. Their long, pointed noses give them an excellent sense of smell. Mongooses

The Liberian mongoose uses its long nose to smell prey, which it digs out of the ground with its claws.

constantly put their noses to the ground as they hunt for prey. Prey that is close by or does not move is found almost entirely by smell. Mongooses also frequently stand tall and sniff the air to help them locate prey and predators that are farther away.

Two kinds of African mongooses, the Liberian mongoose and the cusimanse, use their noses for more than smelling. These mongooses have extra-long, trunklike noses. As these mongooses dig with their claws, they use their noses to help move away the soil.

For locating distant prey, mongooses also have excellent hearing. The small, rounded ears of mongooses are almost hidden in their thick fur. Mongooses can even fold their ears to keep dirt from getting in them while **burrowing**.

Mongooses have good vision, and some can see colors. Their vision is especially important for locating prey and enemies that move. Mongooses that hunt out in the open during the day need keen eyesight to see birds of prey that present a constant danger. The daytime-hunting meerkats have such keen eyes that they can spot a hawk when it is only a speck in the sky to a human eye.

Besides sight, smell, and hearing, mongooses also have special whiskers to help them locate prey. These long, thick hairs are very sensitive to touch. They are called **vibrissae**. Mongooses have these hairs on their lips, in the corner of their mouths, on their cheeks, above their eyes, and on their wrists.

Teeth and Diet

Mongooses have thirty-four to forty strong teeth in a powerful jaw. Like other mammal carnivores, most mongooses have four long, sharp **canine teeth**. They are used to grip and bite prey. Mongooses also have two pairs of teeth that work like scissors. These slice up mice, lizards, and other prey for easier swallowing. The fierce slender mongoose has some of the largest slicing teeth. Mongooses also have **molars** with sharp points for crunching hard shells of prey such as beetles, scorpions, and crabs. These molars are especially strong in mongooses that eat mostly insects, such as the meerkats of southern Africa.

Anne Rasa, a scientist who studied dwarf mongooses for several years in Africa, experienced first-hand the strong bite of the mongoose. When a dwarf mongoose grabbed her finger with its teeth, she had to use a knife to force open the animal's locked jaws.

Mongoose Anatomy

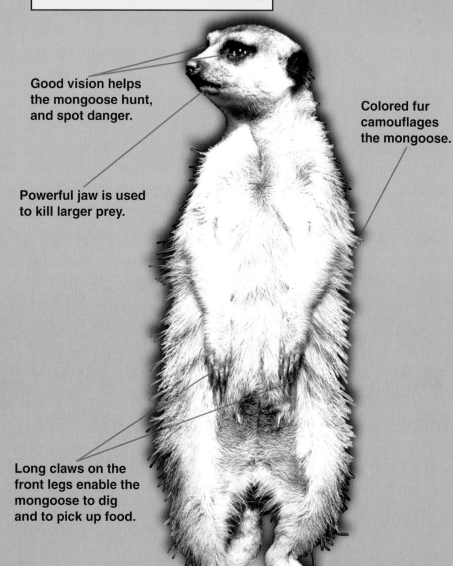

Good vision helps the mongoose hunt, and spot danger.

Colored fur camouflages the mongoose.

Powerful jaw is used to kill larger prey.

Long claws on the front legs enable the mongoose to dig and to pick up food.

Strong legs allow the mongoose to move quickly when hunting.

Mongooses are not fussy eaters. They generally eat whatever prey they can find that is smaller than they are. The most carnivorous mongooses, such as the Egyptian mongoose, eat mostly small animals such as rats, mice, lizards, snakes, and birds. But they also eat smaller prey such as insects, spiders, and scorpions. Small mongooses, such as the dwarf mongooses and meerkats, eat mostly insects, spiders, and other small prey. But these small mongooses also use their strong bites and powerful jaws to kill larger prey, such as mice and lizards, when the opportunity arises. Sometimes, smaller mongooses work together to kill a larger prey such as a snake. Mongooses also eat the eggs of birds and other animals.

Mongooses are unusual in that they eat many kinds of prey that other predators avoid, such as poisonous snakes, slimy frogs, and stinging scorpions. Because mongooses eat such a wide range of prey, they are less dependent on a particular habitat than many other predators. In fact, the food of the same species may differ greatly depending on where it lives. For example, the small Indian mongoose usually eats small animals such as rats. In some places in Hawaii, where this mongoose was introduced in 1883, it eats mostly crabs and fish. These prey are more plentiful in the islands.

The mongoose's sharp senses, agile body, and lightning-quick reflexes make it a highly successful predator wherever it lives.

CHAPTER TWO

Lone and Group Hunters

Mongooses are aggressive, active hunters. Some kinds hunt alone, others in groups. Most hunt by day, but some are active at night. Whatever a mongoose's hunting style, it is a fierce predator. With its quick, agile movements; lightning-fast, strong bite; and keen senses; prey rarely stand a chance.

Lone Hunters

Most mongooses are solitary hunters. They usually hunt alone. Some examples are the slender mongoose, the Indian gray mongoose, and the small Indian mongoose. The most carnivorous mongooses tend to be solitary. They feed primarily on small animals such as mice, lizards, and snakes. To capture such prey, a mongoose must approach quietly and unseen. This is done most successfully alone.

The slender mongoose of Africa is a very successful lone hunter. It lives in forests and **savannas**. True to its name, this mongoose is very thin and is one of the smallest solitary hunters. It has a speckled coat, ranging from yellowish to dark brown, a black-tipped tail, and red eyes.

Like most solitary hunters, the slender mongoose searches for prey primarily during the daytime in places with plant cover for hiding from prey and predators. The slender mongoose trots silently through the forest or the tall grasses of the savanna. It hunts with its head down, its legs crouched, and its tail trailing behind, smelling and looking for prey. From time to time it stops and stands upright to peer above the plant

A slender mongoose hunts for food on a termite mound. Slender mongooses prefer to hunt alone.

Dwarf mongooses are social hunters. They work together to find food.

growth and sniff the air. When the mongoose flushes a mouse or lizard from hiding, it either pounces on the prey or chases after it. Once the prey is cornered, the mongoose grabs it with strong jaws.

Group Hunters

Some kinds of mongooses band together into large family groups or clans to hunt. Mongooses that live and hunt in groups are called **social** mongooses. Some examples are dwarf mongooses, banded mongooses, and meerkats. All of these live in Africa.

Social mongooses tend to share several characteristics. They are often small creatures that eat mostly insects and hunt by day in the open. Insects are often plentiful in the grasslands and other open areas of Africa where these mongooses hunt. By hunting in groups, the mongooses are able to take advantage of this rich food supply and still stay safe. Mongooses, especially small ones hunting in the open, are in constant danger from birds of prey. Hunting in a group provides lots of eyes, ears, and noses to spot danger.

The meerkat is perhaps the best known of the group hunters. It is gray or tan, with brown bands on its back and a slim, rather than bushy, tail. Its ears, nose, patches around its eyes, and tip of its tail are black. Meerkats live and hunt in some of the driest and most open country in southern Africa.

In the morning a group of as many as thirty meerkats sets out to hunt a short distance from their burrow. The group spreads out and each meerkat searches for prey on its own. They keep in touch by sight and constant murmuring. As each meerkat crawls along, its nose constantly sniffs the ground for buried

The meerkat is a type of mongoose that lives in the dry, open country of southern Africa.

prey such as insects or their **larvae**. Unlike the slender mongoose that moves swiftly along as it hunts, the meerkat stops to scratch in every hole, **crevice**, and cranny. When it smells a prey, it digs rapidly with its long, strong claws. The meerkat has especially large front claws, which make it an excellent digger. It can move sand equal to its own weight in seconds to uncover a fat beetle larva. Once the larva is uncovered, the meerkat grabs it with the jaws of its pointed snout.

Water Hunters

Though most mongooses hunt prey on the ground, some hunt in water. Others hunt near water. These **semiaquatic** mongooses include the marsh mongoose of Africa and the crab-eating and short-tailed mongooses of Asia. Most semiaquatic mongooses hunt at night. They eat mostly freshwater crabs, frogs, and fish.

The marsh mongoose is the most at home in the water. It is large and sturdy with a shaggy, dark-brown coat. This type of mongoose lives in swamps, marshes, and other wet areas of Africa. It swims and dives much like an otter.

The marsh mongoose hunts by wading into shallow water at nightfall. It searches underwater for crayfish, mussels, snails, fish, frogs, and insects. This type of mongoose finds its prey by feeling with its hands on the muddy bottom, under rocks, and in crevices. It has long, sensitive fingers and naked, soft palms adapted for feeling hidden prey. Other mongooses, including those that hunt on land, have webbing between their

The sensitive fingers of a marsh mongoose help it to find prey hidden underwater.

toes to help them swim. But the marsh mongoose does not. Without the webbing the marsh mongoose can spread its fingers wide to find prey.

A hunting marsh mongoose wades back and forth through a pool of water, feeling the bottom as it goes. It cannot see what it is doing because it keeps its head above water. When the mongoose finds a fish or other prey, it rears up and pulls its catch out of the water. It then uses its fingers to put the prey in its mouth. In addition to hunting underwater, the marsh mongoose also travels on regular paths along the edges of streams and marshes to find food. There it uses its long fingers to grab crabs out of holes in the muddy banks.

Other Night Hunters

Besides the mongooses that hunt in water, a few other species hunt mainly at night. One is the Meller's mongoose. Its favorite food is harvester termites. These termites live in underground nests in Africa's grasslands and only come out at night to eat. Another night hunter is the white-tailed mongoose. Like the social mongooses, this mongoose hunts primarily insects in the open plains of Africa and southern Arabia. But unlike the group hunters, it is solitary. By hunting at night, it avoids most of the predators that threaten group hunters during the day.

The white-tailed mongoose has a long neck and legs, and usually a bushy, white tail. It has been called Africa's version of a skunk. After the sun sets, the white-tailed mongoose leaves its den and zigzags through open grassland. One of its favorite places to

The white-tailed mongoose is a clever hunter that sometimes uses tricks to catch its prey.

hunt is where huge herds of zebras, gazelles, and other animals graze. The herds leave behind piles of **dung**, which attract dung beetles. The mongoose digs through the dung with its long claws to uncover these beetles and their larvae.

Tricky Hunters

The white-tailed mongoose sometimes uses tricks to lure its prey. On moonlit nights it has been seen dancing, and waving its bushy, white tail in front of a henhouse. The dancing arouses the curiosity of the chickens, which watch through the wire fence around the henhouse. If a chicken sticks its head through a hole in the fence to get a closer look, the mongoose quickly bites off its head.

Like the white-tailed mongoose, the Egyptian mongoose uses various acts to lure birds. Sometimes this mongoose chases its tail or twitches the tail's black tip. These actions make birds curious. When they come close to investigate, the mongoose grabs them. In another trick, the mongoose rears up on its back legs, then flops over. Curious birds come closer. The mongoose rolls around, getting closer and closer to the birds. Suddenly, it lunges and grabs the birds in its jaws.

Mongooses are highly successful hunters. Alone or in groups, they are experts at finding a wide variety of prey: rats, mice, lizards, scorpions, spiders, eggs, insects, and insect larvae. Once a mongoose sniffs a possible meal, the prey best beware. The mongoose pursues its prey aggressively. Before long, the quick, agile mongoose has the prey in its grip.

CHAPTER THREE

The Bite and the Feast

An insect or mouse caught in the sharp claws or strong jaws of a mongoose has little chance of escape. With a fierce bite, the mongoose kills its prey with sharp canine teeth, then chops or crunches it.

Mongooses kill most prey with a lightning-quick, strong bite to the neck or head. Large prey, such as mice and lizards, are most often killed with a bite to the neck at the back of the skull. Insects and other small prey are usually bitten on the head. Either kind of bite smashes the prey's skull, killing the animal. Sometimes mongooses bite their prey fiercely several times, even after the prey stops moving.

Some mongooses also shake their prey violently from side to side to help kill it. The dwarf mongoose, which bites all of its prey on the head, shakes large prey, such as a grass rat. Dwarf mongooses and

A yellow mongoose kills a snake with a bite to its head.

meerkats shake small prey, such as centipedes and lizards, that are likely to grab their snouts. The shaking keeps the prey from getting a grip and also helps kill it.

Special Handling

Prey that is poisonous or dangerous may get special handling before being eaten. For example, when the small Indian mongoose captures a scorpion or centipede, it not only bites the prey but tosses it

This meerkat has captured a scorpion, which will soon become a meal.

repeatedly until it stops moving. When a dwarf mongoose meets a scorpion in Africa's dry bush, it first bites off the prey's claws. Only then does it kill the scorpion. The dwarf mongoose shows no concern regarding the scorpion's poisonous stinger. Mongooses are too fast to be stung by a scorpion. Sometimes the dwarf mongoose even eats the stinger without worrying about the poison within it.

Meerkats are more cautious with their prey than most mongooses. As meerkats comb the dry plains of southern Africa, they often dig their prey from deep in the ground. There, dangerous prey, such as scorpions, can hide. So meerkats are careful. They wait until a prey is completely out of the ground before they even attempt to bite it. That way prey that is dangerous, large, or unfamiliar can first be battered with the claws before being snapped at with the meerkat's teeth. Only after all this does the meerkat give the prey a hard bite and a shake.

Cracking Open Hard Prey

Large eggs and other hard-shelled prey need to be cracked open before they can be eaten. Mongooses do this in two main ways. The marsh mongoose, which eats mostly prey with hard shells such as mussels, crabs, and crocodile eggs, uses the first method. This type of mongoose stands on its hind legs with the object in its front paws. It then hurls the prey against a rock or the ground to break it open. A marsh mongoose's favorite stone near a river or lake often will be littered with shells.

A banded mongoose digs in the dry ground in search of insects.

The slender and the Egyptian mongooses are among those that crack open prey the second way. A mongoose using this method rolls or carries the egg or other hard-shelled prey to a tree, wall, or rock. The mongoose turns its back to the tree, wall, or rock, spreads its hind legs, and flings the object between its hind legs against the hard surface. It then springs around and eats the contents of the broken object. The banded mongoose and the cape gray mongoose are among those that use both methods at different times.

The Feast

Once a prey has been killed, mongooses may carry it to a safe place to eat it. Egyptian mongooses, found from Africa to southern Europe, sometimes go inside deep shrubbery to eat their prey. The social mongooses of Africa eat insect prey on the spot. But they often carry larger prey, such as rats, to a protected spot so another pack member cannot steal their food. A **termite mound** is sometimes used as a hiding place.

Mongooses eat their prey by cutting and chopping it up with their

Mongooses feast on large prey, like this deadly King Cobra, from the head down.

Two adult banded mongooses and their litter hunt for food in a termite mound.

sharp teeth. Insect prey is often merely crunched up, especially by strong back teeth. Large prey is eaten from the head down. For example, a slender mongoose eating a mouse in the forest or savanna of Africa starts with the head. The mongoose then eats down into the body of the mouse, without skinning it. The mongoose eats through everything—even the bones. Not a scrap of meat is wasted. If any bits of food get stuck in its teeth, the mongoose removes them with the claws of its front feet. All that is left when the

Adult mongooses bring food to their dens to feed their young.

mongoose is done is a small strip of furry skin, the tail, and the feet. Likewise, when eating a bird, all that remains is a few large feathers.

Some mongooses hold prey with their front claws while they rip it up. The meerkat does this with large prey such as mice, lizards, and birds. First the meerkat lifts the head of the prey with its jaws. Then it presses the rest of the prey's body to the ground with its front paws. To rip the prey apart, the meerkat pulls down on it with its claws while pulling up with its jaws. Little by little, the prey is torn into bits and swallowed.

To Share or Not to Share

Mongooses are usually extremely protective of their food while eating. The meerkat is a good example of this behavior. Even when meerkats are full, they will try to steal food from one another as they hunt on the dry plains or savannas of southern Africa. To keep food from being stolen, a meerkat drags it away from the pack. If several meerkats approach one that is eating, the lone meerkat will rapidly turn its back on the thieves while keeping its front feet on the prey. The meerkat may even lie across its prey to keep it from being stolen. The banded mongoose jumps at food thieves with angry squeals and growls.

On the other hand, adult mongooses readily share their food with youngsters. In Africa's social mongoose groups, even adults not related to babies give them food. When babies are very young, adults bring food back to the den for them. Later, adults share food with youngsters old enough to join the hunting group.

In dwarf mongoose packs, food also is shared with the queen and the dominant male. Dwarf mongoose packs are unique in that only one female queen and one male have all the babies. These adults have priority over food captured by any member of the group at any time.

Mongooses are very skillful and efficient both at killing and eating their prey. Not only are they able to consume an amazing variety of prey, but they waste next to nothing. Mongooses are not likely to go hungry.

CHAPTER FOUR

Staying Safe from Enemies

As one of the smallest carnivores, mongooses are preyed on by many enemies. Predators include **jackals**, **servals**, hyenas, snakes, and dogs. Mongooses also are in danger from many birds of prey, such as eagles and hawks.

By keeping hidden, mongooses stay safe when they are not hunting. They rest in burrows, caves, rock piles, termite mounds, and other hideouts. The dwarf mongoose of southern Africa has found a way to make its hideout even safer. It often places its den near a bee or wasp nest. The stinging insects keep intruders away.

Another way mongooses hide from eagles and other predators is by their coloring. Mongooses usually have gray or brown coats, to blend in with the soil or trees where they hunt. Some mongooses have different colors depending on where they hunt. For example, the slender mongoose has a yellow-brown coat in dry areas of Africa and a dark brown coat in forests.

Guards and Babysitters

The social mongooses of Africa are in the most danger when they hunt. Because they hunt in the open with their noses buried in the ground, they are easy targets. To keep safe, most social mongooses post guards to watch for birds of prey and other predators.

A meerkat guard stands on its back legs on a high rock or mound of earth so it can see farther. If a guard sees a predator with its sharp eyes, it warns the group. A long howl signals a bird of prey. A gruff *waauk-waauk*

The mongoose has many enemies, including the African leopard.

Meerkats post guards when they hunt, to warn others when predators are near.

warns of a land predator such as a jackal. Hearing the warning signal, the group stops hunting and dashes for cover.

Dwarf mongooses also post guards, but sometimes get extra help from birds. Dwarf mongooses team up with birds called hornbills, which act as lookouts. In the morning the birds gather near termite mounds where dwarf mongooses spend the night. When the mongooses come out, they and the birds set out to hunt together. The birds catch grasshoppers and mice flushed out by the mongooses. In return, the hornbills warn the mongooses of predators, especially birds of prey.

Dashing for Cover

When mongooses spot a predator, the best defense is to run for cover. Mongooses often hunt close to their hideouts, so they do not have far to go. Even though most mongooses have short legs, many can run fast for short distances. When a bird of prey is spotted, the mongooses immediately dash for cover. However, when mongooses sense a land predator, like a jackal, they often first stand upright to find the predator's exact location. Then they can choose the best path to avoid the intruder.

The marsh mongoose escapes African land predators, such as hyenas, by diving into water. It can stay underwater for a long time with only its nose sticking above the surface. The slender mongoose, one of the few mongooses that can climb, often flees up a tree to avoid predators.

Fighting Snakes

When a mongoose and a snake meet, the mongoose does not have to run away. In a fight with a snake, the mongoose almost always wins because of its greater speed and agility. The mongoose's quick movements allow it to jump out of reach of the snake's strike.

One of the most famous snake fighters is the Indian gray mongoose of Asia, which tangles with the deadly cobra. Upon finding a cobra the mongoose jumps around the snake trying to get it to strike. Then, when the snake strikes, the mongoose jumps quickly aside. The mongoose does this again and again, tiring the snake. Finally, when the snake lowers its head to strike one last time, the mongoose pounces on it from above. The mongoose cracks the snake's skull with one bite.

The cobra is a deadly snake, but it is no match for the fast and agile mongoose.

The mongoose uses its speed to tire a cobra, then delivers a deadly bite to the head.

If the mongoose should get bitten when fighting a snake, it will not die. Snake **venom** is not as harmful to mongooses as it is to most animals. For example, a mongoose can survive six times the dose of venom that would kill a rabbit.

Bluffing the Enemy

While mongooses can kill snakes, they are too small to win fights against larger predators, such as jackals. For that reason mongooses use elaborate bluffs when they are surprised or corned away from their hideouts. To scare off enemies the mongooses make themselves look much bigger and fiercer than they really are. They do this by straightening their legs, arching their backs, and bristling their fur. To add to the trick, they open their mouths wide and growl, snap, and spit.

In Africa the banded mongooses and meerkats take the bluff even further. The whole pack clusters together in a mock mobbing attack. Every animal jumps, rocks, and runs in place while bristling their fur and growling. The pack looks like a single large, angry animal galloping toward the enemy. In reality, the pack is hardly moving. The growling mob, though, is usually successful in scaring off a jackal or serval.

Stinky Spray

Animals that attack a mongoose also may be squirted with a stinky liquid. Mongooses that can spray foul-smelling fluid include the white-tailed and the marsh mongooses of Africa and the crab-eating mongooses of Asia. The foul-smelling liquid is produced in glands near a mongoose's tail.

A dwarf mongoose shows its sharp teeth to scare off a predator.

Before squirting its fluid, the white-tailed mongoose arches, fluffs, and waves its tail as a warning. This is usually enough to scare spotted hyenas and other predators away. But if they persist, they get a dose of stinky-smelling spray that sends them on their way.

Mongooses and People

In most places mongooses live, people consider them friends because they keep rodent and snake populations under control. However, in a few places, people view mongooses as pests. In the late 1800s small Indian mongooses were taken to Jamaica, Hawaii, and other places to control the many rats on sugarcane plantations. As the rat population decreased, though, mongooses turned to other prey. They caused a great deal of damage to farm animals and rare species such as the Jamaica petrel, a seabird. For that reason it is now illegal to bring mongooses into the United States and some other parts of the world. The small Indian mongooses that remained in these places have been hunted as pests. But they continue to survive and thrive despite people's efforts.

In India, on the other hand, gray mongooses, also known as common mongooses, are rapidly declining in number. This is due to illegal trade in mongoose hair. Their hair is used to make artists' paintbrushes. To gather enough hair to make the brushes, thousands of mongooses are illegally killed each year. Wildlife experts say many people all over the world that use the brushes do not know what they are made from.

Mongoose Prey

• Scorpion

• Spider

• Beetle

• Lizard

• Bird eggs

Mongooses are also in danger elsewhere. Several species of mongooses are listed as threatened by the International Union for Conservation of Nature and Natural Resources. These mongooses are on the list because they are in danger of dying out unless steps are taken to protect them. Five of the species on the list live only on Madagascar, a large island off the southeast coast of Africa. The Madagascar species in the most danger are the narrow-striped mongoose and the giant-striped mongoose.

The biggest threat to the Madagascar mongooses is that their habitat is being destroyed. In the two thousand years since people came to the island, around 90 percent of its forestland have disappeared. The remaining forests continue to be destroyed at an alarming rate of 370,000 to 490,000 acres per year. Mostly, the forests are being burned to clear land for farming, or cut down to provide firewood and building materials. Many groups worldwide are working to save the island's forests. They provide homes for hundreds of animals and plants that live nowhere else in the world. The goal is to find ways for the people of this poor country to make a living without destroying the forestland. Progress is being made, but much is left to be done.

Overall, mongooses are highly adaptable and continue to thrive in many environments. They may be small, but they are fierce and mighty. These alert, quick-moving hunters are among the most formidable predators on Earth.

GLOSSARY

adapted: Made fit for surviving in a specific environment.

burrowing: Digging a tunnel in the ground.

burrows: Tunnels under the ground used for shelter.

canine teeth: Long, pointed teeth carnivores use to grab, bite, and rip prey.

Carnivora: Classification of mammals that are adapted for hunting, killing, and eating the flesh of other animals.

crevice: Narrow opening.

dung: Solid waste of an animal.

habitats: The natural homes of plants or animals.

jackals: Animals of Africa and Asia that look like small dogs.

larvae: Baby insects, which often have soft bodies and look like worms.

mammals: Animals that nurse their young with milk from mammary glands.

molars: Large teeth at the back of the mouth used for crunching prey.

predator: An animal that hunts other animals for food.

prey: An animal hunted by another animal for food.

savannas: Flat, grassy plains that have only a few trees.

semiaquatic: Living in water part of the time.

servals: African wildcats that have huge ears, long legs, and a light-brown coat with black spots.

social: Living together in an organized commmunity.

species: A group of animals or plants that share similar characteristics and can reproduce.

termite mound: Large earthen nest built by colonies of small, white insects called termites.

venom: Liquid poison produced by some animals.

vibrissae: Long, stiff hairs or whiskers that are very sensitive to touch.

➤ FOR FURTHER EXPLORATION ◄

Books (Nonfiction)

Maurice Burton and Robert Burton, Ed. *International Wildlife Encyclopedia*. Tarrytown, NY: Marshall Cavendish, 2002. The characteristics and behaviors of the mongoose family are described in this reference on wildlife around the world.

Erin Pembrey Swan, *Land Predators Around the World*. New York: Franklin Watts, 2001. This book describes the traits of predators around the world. The marsh mongoose and meerkat are among the many featured.

Jenny Tesar, *What on Earth is a Meerkat?* Woodbridge, CT: Blackbirch Press, 1994. In full-page colorful photos and easy-to-read text, this book describes the meerkat and its way of life. Topics covered include what meerkats look like, where they live, what they eat, how they reproduce, and how they survive.

Books (Fiction)

Rudyard Kipling, *Rikki-Tikki-Tavi*. Adapt. Jerry Pinkney. New York: Morrow Junior Books, 1997. Part of Rudyard Kipling's novel *The Jungle Book*, this story tells of a fearless pet mongoose that fights two cobras to protect the life of its young master.

Periodicals

Jane R. McCauley, "Make Way for the Mongoose," *National Geographic World*, June 1995.

Ranger Rick, "Don't Mess with a Mongoose," January 1998.

Video

Meerkats United, Shanachie Entertainment, 1995. Originally a PBS Nature series program, this video shows meerkats working as a team to survive in the Kalahari Desert in South Africa. Guard duty, babysitting, and hunting are featured.

Web Sites

Animal Planet: Meerkats Unmasked (http://animal.discovery.com). This site features moving pictures of meerkats waking up, climbing a small tree, and digging for lunch. It also includes photos and descriptions of several other mongoose behaviors, such as burrowing and grooming. Close-up views of the meerkat's body also are featured.

Enchanted Learning: African Animals Coloring/Info Pages (www.enchantedlearning.com). This site features information and coloring pages about many African animals, including the yellow mongoose and the meerkat.

Minnesota Zoo: Meerkats of the Kalahari (www.mnzoo.com). This site features information and photos about meerkats that live in the Kalahari Desert in southern Africa. The site includes a map of the desert and discusses what it is like to live there.

Safaricamlive: Southern African Mammals (www.safaricamlive.com). This site on African wildlife provides photos and information for several mongooses. Featured are the banded, dwarf, slender, water, and yellow mongooses. Information is given on habitat, diet, behavior, and predators.

INDEX

PICTURE CREDITS

ABOUT THE AUTHOR

Author Janet Halfmann has written many nonfiction books for children and young adults, most of them on animals and nature. Her books include a six-title series on wildlife habitats, and several books on the lives and behavior of insects and spiders. This book is her third in the KidHaven Nature's Predators series.

The wonders of nature have intrigued Halfmann from the time she was a child growing up on a farm in Michigan. She is a former daily newspaper reporter, children's magazine managing editor, and children's activity book writer and managing editor. When she is not writing, Halfmann works in her garden, explores nature, and spends time with her family.